THE MATHEMATICIAN WHO PREDICTED COMPUTERS

THE STORY OF ADA LOVELACE FOR KIDS

JAMES SMITH

BOOKSTEM

CONTENTS

1

A BRILLIANT BEGINNING

Introduction to Ada Lovelace

Ada Lovelace had a way of seeing the world that was completely different from most people around her. While others saw machines as simple tools, Ada saw something much more exciting—something almost alive with possibilities. Numbers weren't just numbers to her. They were ideas, connections, even music.

She wasn't supposed to be this way. At least, that's what her mother had hoped.

Ada was born in 1815 into a famous family. Her father, Lord Byron, was one of the most well-known poets of the time, known for writing dramatic verses and living an even more dramatic life. But he wasn't around for very long. Just a few weeks after Ada was born, he left England and never came back. That meant Ada grew up with her mother, Lady Byron, who had strong opinions about how her daughter should be raised.

Lady Byron didn't want Ada to follow in her father's footsteps. Poetry? No. Wild emotions? Definitely not. She believed that logic and reason were the way to a proper life. Instead of letting Ada get lost in stories and daydreams, she surrounded her with math and science. Her tutors drilled her in numbers and equations, and she was expected to study hard.

But something unexpected happened.

Instead of resisting math, Ada loved it. She didn't just learn equations—she played with them, turning numbers into patterns and puzzles in her mind. Where others saw rules and limits, Ada saw adventure. Even as a child, she asked questions that no one had thought to ask before. Could numbers be used to create pictures? Could machines think beyond simple calculations? Could they be taught to create?

Ada's mind didn't fit neatly into a single category. She was fascinated by science but also drawn to art. She once designed a plan to build a flying machine, carefully studying the way birds moved to figure out how wings should work. She sketched out diagrams, took notes, and imagined a world where people could glide through the air like birds. This wasn't just a daydream—it was a carefully thought-out experiment, based on research and observation. She was only twelve.

It wasn't always easy. In the 1800s, girls weren't expected to study subjects like math and engineering. Many people believed that women didn't have the kind of minds suited for that kind of work. They thought girls should focus on things like sewing, music, and running a household. But Ada had no interest in those things. She wanted to explore, to learn, to create.

And she was lucky—she had people in her life who saw her potential. Her mother made sure she had excellent teachers, including some of the best mathematicians of the time. One of them, a man named Augustus De Morgan, was amazed by how quickly Ada understood complicated ideas. He even told her mother that Ada could be one of the great mathematical minds of the time—if she had been born a boy, that is.

But Ada didn't let other people's opinions stop her. She kept pushing forward, eager to learn more.

She wanted to understand how things worked—not just on the surface, but deep down.

That curiosity led her to someone who would change her life: Charles Babbage.

Babbage was an inventor, a thinker, and a bit of a troublemaker when it came to challenging the way things were done. He had a bold idea—a machine that could solve complex mathematical problems automatically. At the time, calculations had to be done by hand, which meant they took a long time and could be full of mistakes. Babbage believed a machine could do it faster and more accurately.

He called it the Difference Engine. It was a machine made of gears and levers, built to crunch numbers with precision. To most people, it looked like a fancy clockwork contraption. To Ada, it looked like the beginning of something much bigger.

The first time she saw it, something clicked in her mind. While others saw a complicated piece of machinery, Ada saw potential. If a machine could follow instructions to calculate numbers, what else could it do? Could it be taught to follow more complex instructions? Could it think in a way that was almost human?

She started asking questions that no one else had asked before. Not even Babbage.

The two of them became fast friends. Babbage was impressed by Ada's sharp mind, and he enjoyed talking to someone who understood his ideas. Ada, in turn, was fascinated by his work and wanted to help make his machines a reality. She became deeply involved in his next invention—an even more advanced machine called the Analytical Engine.

While the Difference Engine could only solve specific types of problems, the Analytical Engine was designed to be more flexible. It could be programmed to follow different instructions, making it more like a modern computer. But there was a problem—no one had figured out how to actually write those instructions yet.

That was where Ada came in.

She didn't just study Babbage's designs—she expanded on them. She saw possibilities that even he hadn't considered. While he focused on numbers, Ada saw something more: a machine that could process information in entirely new ways. She believed that, given the right instructions, it could do much more than just math. It could compose music, analyze patterns, and maybe even create.

She was describing something that didn't exist yet—a world where machines could be more than just calculators. A world where computers, as we know them today, might one day exist.

Most people couldn't understand what she was talking about. Even Babbage himself didn't completely see what she saw. But Ada kept working, kept writing, kept explaining. She wrote the very first detailed instructions for how a machine like the Analytical Engine could be programmed—a set of instructions that would later be recognized as the first true computer program.

At the time, very few people paid attention to her work. Machines like Babbage's were expensive to build, and many believed they weren't practical. The Analytical Engine was never fully constructed during their lifetimes. But Ada's notes remained, waiting for the right time to be rediscovered.

Born into a famous family

Byron wasn't the kind of man who followed rules. He was a celebrity before celebrities even existed, known for his daring travels, scandalous romances, and bold opinions. Some people called him a genius. Others thought he was reckless. One thing was certain—he was always the center of attention.

But there was one thing he didn't stick around for: fatherhood.

Ada never really knew her father. Just a few weeks after she was born, he left England and never came back. He didn't hold her in his arms, didn't see her take her first steps, didn't teach her a single thing. The only connection she had to him was through his poetry and the stories people told.

Her mother, Lady Byron, made sure those stories weren't particularly kind.

Lady Byron and Lord Byron had one of the most dramatic marriages of their time. It didn't last long—just over a year—and ended in anger and bitterness. No one knows exactly what happened behind closed doors, but whatever it was, it convinced Lady Byron to take baby Ada and leave for good.

And she didn't just leave. She made sure that Ada would never become anything like her father.

Lady Byron believed that Lord Byron's poetry-filled, emotional nature was dangerous. To her, poetry meant chaos, and chaos meant trouble. She wanted Ada to be logical, disciplined, and steady—nothing like the man who had caused her so much pain. That's why she made sure Ada's education was filled with math and science instead of poetry and art.

But here's the strange part—Ada did take after her father, just not in the way her mother feared. She didn't run off on wild adventures or write dramatic poems about lost love. But she did have a huge imagination, a deep curiosity about the world, and a mind that refused to follow ordinary paths.

She saw things differently than other people.

Even numbers, something most people thought of as cold and lifeless, felt alive to her. She could look at an equation and see beauty in it, the same way someone else might see beauty in a poem. Her mind worked in patterns and connections, blending logic with creativity.

That combination—math and imagination—was exactly what made her special.

If she had only been a mathematician, she might have become a great scholar, but she wouldn't have thought about machines the way she did. If she had only been a dreamer, she might have written stories, but she wouldn't have developed the first ideas of computer programming. She needed both sides of her mind to do what no one else had done before.

In a way, Lady Byron's strict approach backfired. Instead of erasing Lord Byron's influence, she helped shape Ada into something completely new—not a poet, not just a mathematician, but something in between.

Even though Ada never met her father, she was always curious about him. She read his poetry, even though her mother didn't approve. She wanted to know who he really was—not just the wild stories people told, but the person behind them.

And there was something else.

She wondered what he would have thought of her.

Her mother wanted Ada to focus on math and science

Lady Byron believed numbers were safe. Numbers followed rules. They didn't change their minds or run off on reckless adventures. Unlike poetry, which could stir up wild emotions, math was steady, logical, and disciplined. And discipline was exactly what she wanted for Ada.

She had seen firsthand what happened when someone lived by emotion instead of reason. Her husband, Lord Byron, had been passionate, unpredictable, and impossible to control. His words could move people to tears, but his actions left chaos in their wake. She had no interest in raising a daughter who would follow in those footsteps.

To prevent that, she built Ada's world around logic.

Ada's lessons began early. Other children might have spent their time playing, but Ada was given tutors, strict schedules, and demanding subjects. While most girls her age learned embroidery and music, Ada was studying arithmetic, geometry, and even astronomy. If her mother had anything to say about it, her daughter would grow up to be a thinker, not a dreamer.

But there was one problem.

Ada was both.

She didn't just memorize equations—she explored them. She didn't just follow instructions —she asked questions no one expected. And while her mother had done everything in her power to keep Ada's education grounded in logic, she couldn't stop Ada from seeing the world differently.

Even math, the very subject that was supposed to be solid and predictable, became something more in Ada's mind. She saw numbers as more than just tools for solving problems. To her, they were like a secret language, full of patterns waiting to be uncovered. Equations weren't just answers—they were ideas.

That was something her mother hadn't counted on.

Lady Byron wanted Ada to think like a scientist, and she did. But she also thought like an artist. Even when she was working with numbers, her imagination refused to stay quiet.

At one point, she became fascinated with the idea of flying. Not just as a passing thought, but as a real scientific possibility. She studied the wings of birds, making careful notes about how they moved through the air. She sketched out designs for a flying machine, complete with calculations about how it might work. She wasn't just dreaming about flying— she was trying to figure out how to make it happen.

This was exactly the kind of thinking that made Ada different.

Her mother had given her the tools of logic and reason, but she used them in ways no one expected. Where others might see a problem and work out a solution, Ada saw a possibility and asked, "What else can this do?"

That way of thinking would shape everything she did.

As she grew older, her studies became even more

intense. Most girls of her time never studied advanced mathematics, but Ada was different. She worked with some of the best mathematicians of the time, including Augustus De Morgan, a professor who was astonished by her ability to grasp complex ideas. He even wrote to her mother, saying that Ada's mind was as sharp as any man's—something that was rarely said about women in those days.

But Ada wasn't just good at math. She wanted to push it further, to connect it to things no one else had considered.

Ada's early interest in numbers and machines

Numbers weren't just something Ada learned in school. They were something she played with, something she saw everywhere. While other children might have spent their afternoons running through fields or playing with dolls, Ada was busy solving puzzles, asking questions, and trying to understand the world through patterns.

To her, math wasn't a list of problems to be solved. It was a way to uncover secrets hiding beneath the surface of everything. She saw numbers in music, in the rhythm of footsteps, in the way the stars moved across the night sky. Even machines—

gears, levers, pulleys—were full of numbers and rules that made them work.

She wanted to understand those rules.

By the time she was eight, Ada was already developing a deep fascination with how things functioned. She would take apart objects just to figure out how they were put together. Clocks, toys, even household gadgets—if it had moving parts, Ada wanted to study it. She wasn't trying to break them. She wanted to know why they worked the way they did and whether they could be improved.

This curiosity didn't always go over well with the adults around her. Tutors expected their students to follow lessons, not ask why something worked a certain way. But Ada couldn't help herself. She didn't just want to learn facts—she wanted to dig deeper, to connect ideas in ways no one had before.

One of her earliest obsessions was the idea of building a mechanical horse. She wasn't satisfied with the idea that people had to rely on actual horses for transportation. Couldn't there be another way? Something built, something engineered, something that could move without needing to be fed or rested?

She spent weeks studying how horses walked, observing their legs, sketching different ways gears and wheels might mimic the same motion. To her, it wasn't just a daydream. It was a problem waiting to be solved.

Her mother encouraged the numbers and equations behind these ideas but didn't always know what to make of Ada's way of thinking. Lady Byron had wanted her daughter to be logical and disciplined, but Ada's mind worked in ways that didn't fit neatly into boxes. She wasn't just following the rules of math and science—she was exploring what they could do.

And then, there was her fascination with flying.

Ada was determined to figure out how humans could take to the skies. Not with balloons, which had already been invented, but with something that actually worked the way birds did. She read every book she could find on the subject, collecting ideas from scientists, inventors, and even ancient myths. But books weren't enough.

She needed data.

She observed birds in motion, measuring the angles of their wings and recording how air moved around them. She sketched out plans for winged machines, adjusting them based on what she had learned. She even came up with a name for her research—"flyology."

This was more than just a passing interest. Ada was treating it like a real scientific study. She made detailed calculations, tested ideas, and built theories based on observation. If she had been born in a different time, she might have gone on to design one of the first airplanes.

But something else captured her attention before she could take that idea any further.

Machines.

Ada had always been interested in how things worked, but as she got older, she started thinking about machines in a new way. She wasn't just interested in how gears turned or how pulleys lifted heavy objects. She was interested in what machines could be taught to do.

2

A MIND FOR MACHINES

Most girls in Ada Lovelace's time were not expected to study mathematics. They weren't expected to study much of anything, really—at least not in the way boys did. Education for girls in the early 1800s was usually limited to things that would make them "accomplished," a word that, back then, didn't mean intelligent or knowledgeable. It meant they could play an instrument, stitch embroidery, and maybe speak a little French or Italian to impress guests at a dinner party.

Girls from wealthy families were expected to be graceful, polite, and prepared for marriage. They were taught how to behave in society, how to manage a household, and how to be charming.

Their lessons weren't about logic or problem-solving. They were about refinement.

Ada's education looked nothing like that.

Her mother, Lady Byron, had no interest in raising a daughter who only knew how to play the piano or arrange flowers. She wanted Ada to be sharp, disciplined, and completely uninterested in anything that resembled poetry. To make sure of that, she surrounded her with tutors who focused on math and science.

It was highly unusual. In fact, most people thought it was a waste of time.

Why teach a girl advanced mathematics? Why give her lessons in subjects meant for men? These were the kinds of questions people asked, because they truly believed that certain topics—especially complicated ones—weren't necessary for women to understand.

Ada wasn't concerned with what other people thought.

She was too busy learning.

Her lessons were rigorous, sometimes exhausting, but she didn't resist them. She had a hunger for knowledge, always pushing herself to understand more. She worked with some of the best mathematicians of the time, including Augustus De Morgan, who taught at one of the most prestigious universities in England. He was stunned by how quickly Ada grasped ideas that most people struggled with.

She wasn't just memorizing formulas—she was exploring how numbers worked and what they could do. She asked questions that showed she was thinking beyond the lessons, pushing into new ideas.

Learning mathematics

While most girls her age were learning how to paint delicate watercolors or play the piano to impress future guests, Ada was studying numbers, equations, and theories that even most adults didn't understand. It wasn't just that she was good at math—she was drawn to it, fascinated by the way it explained the world. She could see patterns that others overlooked, and her hunger to understand them only grew stronger as she got older.

Her mother had spared no effort in finding the best teachers, though not all of them knew quite what to do with a student like Ada. Many of them had never taught a girl advanced mathematics before, let alone one who asked questions they had never considered themselves.

One of her most famous teachers was Augustus De Morgan, a brilliant mathematician who taught at University College London. De Morgan was one of the leading experts in algebra and logic, and he quickly realized that Ada was no ordinary student.

Most students—especially beginners—simply memorized mathematical rules and applied them to problems. Ada, on the other hand, wanted to understand why those rules worked. She didn't just accept formulas at face value; she wanted to break them apart and put them back together in different ways.

De Morgan was both impressed and a little taken aback. He had never seen a female student with such a sharp and determined mind. In letters to Lady Byron, he wrote that Ada's ability to grasp complex mathematical ideas was extraordinary, even comparing her to the great thinkers of the past. But then, almost as if he caught himself giving too much praise, he added that this kind of study was more suited to men, as though her talents were somehow misplaced.

Ada didn't care. She kept going, eager to learn more.

Her studies included algebra, calculus, and logic —subjects that were challenging even for the brightest minds. But Ada loved the challenge. She had a way of seeing numbers as more than just tools for solving problems; she saw them as ideas, as structures that could be shaped and expanded in ways most people hadn't even considered.

That kind of thinking made her different.

While many of her tutors focused on teaching her the standard methods, Ada pushed beyond them. She wanted to connect math to other fields—machines, music, even philosophy. She believed numbers could do more than just calculate sums; they could describe patterns in nature, predict outcomes, and even shape the way machines worked.

One of the biggest influences in her life wasn't a teacher in the traditional sense but a scientist and inventor: Charles Babbage.

Babbage was working on something extraordinary—a machine that could perform calculations automatically, almost like a mechanical brain. It was called the Difference Engine, and later, he would begin designing something even more ambitious: the Analytical Engine, a machine that could follow instructions to solve different kinds of problems.

When Ada first met Babbage, she was still a teenager, but she immediately understood the importance of his work. More than that, she saw possibilities in his designs that even he hadn't considered.

Most people looked at Babbage's machines and saw nothing more than a complex way to do arithmetic. Ada saw something revolutionary.

She realized that if a machine could follow a sequence of mathematical steps, it could be programmed. It could go beyond just adding and subtracting—it could process information. She was seeing, decades before anyone else, the beginnings of modern computing.

Her ability to grasp these ideas came from the way she had been trained. Unlike other mathematicians of the time, who saw numbers as separate from the rest of the world, Ada viewed them as part of a larger system. Her education had been different from anyone else's, and because of that, she was able to see what no one else had.

The impact of her mother's encouragement on her studies

Lady Byron was not a warm, affectionate mother. She didn't dote on Ada, didn't fill her childhood with stories and laughter, and certainly didn't encourage whimsy. What she did give her, though, was structure, discipline, and an education unlike any other girl of her time.

While some mothers might have praised their daughters for delicate embroidery or graceful dancing, Lady Byron measured Ada's success by how well she could solve mathematical problems. And Ada, driven by both her own curiosity and the expectations placed upon her, rose to the challenge.

Her mother made sure she had the best tutors, pushing her toward subjects that were considered far too complex for most young girls. She wasn't just learning basic arithmetic—she was tackling advanced algebra, geometry, and even calculus. While other children played simple games, Ada spent hours studying under the watchful eyes of mathematicians and scholars.

There were times when Ada resented the strictness of her education. She was rarely allowed to relax or let her mind wander freely. Every moment had to be productive. If she ever showed signs of what Lady Byron called "poetic tendencies," she was immediately redirected back to the world of numbers and logic.

But while Lady Byron's encouragement came in the form of rigid discipline, it shaped Ada into the thinker she became. Without it, she might never have gained the skills to analyze complex systems or break down ideas into structured patterns—abilities that would later help her understand Charles Babbage's Analytical Engine in a way no one else had.

The constant push toward logic didn't crush Ada's imagination. If anything, it gave her a way to use it differently. Her love for machines, her ability to see numbers as something more than just calculations, and her revolutionary ideas about programming all stemmed from the foundation her mother had built.

She may not have been encouraged to dream, but she was encouraged to think. And thinking—deeply, creatively, and logically—was what would eventually make Ada Lovelace one of the most remarkable minds in history.

3

MEETING CHARLES BABBAGE

Charles Babbage was the kind of man who never stopped thinking. His mind was always turning, always questioning, always searching for a better way to do things. To some, he was a genius. To others, he was a troublemaker who couldn't let go of his impossible ideas. But no matter what people thought of him, one thing was clear—he saw the future long before anyone else did.

Ada Lovelace met Babbage when she was a teenager, but by that time, he was already well known in scientific circles. He wasn't famous in the way poets or politicians were. His name wasn't whispered in gossip salons or printed in newspapers every week. His world was filled with scholars, inventors, and engineers—people who understood how things worked and were determined to push the limits of what was possible.

Babbage had a particular problem he couldn't let go of: human error.

In the early 1800s, numbers ran the world. Banks, businesses, shipping companies, scientists—everyone relied on calculations. But there was a problem. All of those calculations were done by hand, written out by mathematicians or clerks who copied numbers into long tables. And people, no matter how careful, made mistakes.

Babbage hated mistakes.

He once looked at a set of published mathematical tables, the kind used by scientists to calculate measurements, and was horrified by how many errors he found. Some of them were small, but others could lead to serious consequences—wrong calculations in engineering could lead to dangerous failures, and errors in financial records could cost businesses fortunes.

Why, he wondered, did humans have to do all the work? What if a machine could do it instead?

This thought led to what would become his life-long obsession—the Difference Engine.

The Difference Engine was an enormous

mechanical calculator. It used gears, levers, and cranks to automatically perform long, complicated calculations. If built correctly, it would never make mistakes. It would be faster, more reliable, and more efficient than any human mathematician.

Babbage spent years designing and refining his plans. The British government even gave him funding to build it, believing it could revolutionize science and industry. But there was a problem.

The machine was incredibly complicated.

Building something as precise as the Difference Engine required craftsmanship that didn't yet exist. Each tiny gear and lever had to be perfectly made, and technology hadn't caught up with Babbage's ideas. Progress was slow, money ran out, and after years of struggle, the project was never fully completed.

Most people might have stopped there.

Babbage didn't.

Instead, he moved on to an even bigger idea— the Analytical Engine.

Unlike the Difference Engine, which could only perform specific calculations, the Analytical Engine was something entirely new. It wasn't just a calculator. It was programmable.

It could take a set of instructions and follow

them step by step, adjusting as needed. It could store information, make decisions based on inputs, and do more than just add and subtract. It was, in every way, the first concept of a modern computer.

But it was also enormous. If it had ever been built, it would have filled a room. It had thousands of mechanical parts, each one needing to work perfectly with the others. Once again, the technology of the time just wasn't ready for Babbage's vision.

Most people didn't fully understand what he was trying to do. Some thought he was wasting his time. Others believed his ideas were too expensive, too impractical, too ahead of their time to ever be useful.

But Ada Lovelace understood.

When she met Babbage, she wasn't just impressed by the machine. She saw what no one else did—its true potential.

Others looked at the Analytical Engine and saw a machine that could solve equations. Ada saw a machine that could be programmed to do so much more. And because of that, she became the first person to write instructions for a computer—long before computers even existed.

Babbage's machines were never fully built during his lifetime. His ideas faded into history for a time, left in notebooks and sketches that no one thought to take seriously. But more than a hundred years later, when the first real computers were being developed, engineers looked back at his designs and realized something incredible.

Babbage had been right all along.

Ada's fascination with his "Difference Engine"

Ada Lovelace wasn't the only person who had been fascinated by Charles Babbage's Difference Engine. When he first presented the idea to the public, people were eager to see what this machine could do. A device that could calculate numbers without human error? It seemed like magic. Scientists and engineers were impressed, and the British government even funded the project, convinced that it could change the way calculations were done.

But Ada saw something in the Difference Engine that others did not.

The first time she learned about it, she was just a teenager. She had already been studying advanced mathematics, and numbers were something she understood better than most people. But this was something different. A machine that could follow a set of instructions and produce correct results, time after time, without mistakes—this wasn't just a tool. It was something more.

When Ada finally saw the Difference Engine in person, she was completely captivated.

It wasn't like anything else she had ever studied. It wasn't a book of equations or a lesson in logic. It was a physical machine, built with gears and levers, something real and moving. And yet, it followed the same principles she had been learning—patterns, logic, and sequences.

Most people were impressed by the sheer size of it. The machine was made of brass and steel, its gears clicking into place with each calculation. It was large, intricate, and far more complex than any other mechanical device of its time. When Babbage turned the crank, numbers appeared, calculated with perfect accuracy.

But Ada wasn't just watching the machine work. She was thinking about what it meant.

This wasn't just about solving mathematical problems faster. If a machine could be built to follow mathematical instructions, what else could it be built to do?

She asked Babbage questions no one else had thought to ask. Could the machine handle different types of problems? Could it be modified to solve equations that weren't pre-programmed? Could it ever be expanded to do more than just arithmetic?

Babbage, who was used to people admiring his machine but not fully understanding its potential, was surprised. Here was a young woman, still in her teens, who saw beyond the Difference Engine's basic function. She wasn't just looking at what it could do in the present—she was thinking about what machines like it could become.

Their conversation that day was the beginning of an intellectual partnership. Babbage had always been a man of ideas, constantly frustrated by the fact that most people couldn't keep up with him. But Ada could. She not only understood his vision but started expanding on it.

As impressive as the Difference Engine was, Babbage was already working on something even bigger: the Analytical Engine. It was a design that went beyond simple calculations, something that, in theory, could follow a series of instructions to solve different types of problems. It wasn't just a calculator. It was programmable.

And Ada, more than anyone else, understood what that meant.

She became obsessed with the idea—not just of a machine that could compute numbers but of a machine that could follow logic in a way that almost resembled human thought. While others struggled to grasp the significance of Babbage's work, Ada was already thinking about how machines like the Difference Engine and Analytical Engine could be used in ways no one had yet imagined.

Her fascination wasn't just about the technology. It was about the future.

She saw what others couldn't—that machines, if given the right instructions, could do more than just math. They could be programmed to follow patterns, to manipulate symbols, to process information in a way that was eerily similar to human reasoning.

It was an idea that wouldn't be fully understood until the invention of computers over a hundred years later. But for Ada, it was clear even then: machines had the potential to do far more than anyone realized.

Their friendship and collaboration

Ada Lovelace and Charles Babbage were an unlikely pair. He was much older, a well-known scientist with a reputation for being impatient and easily frustrated. She was a young woman in a world where few people believed women had any place in advanced mathematics. And yet, when they talked, there was an instant understanding.

Babbage was used to explaining his ideas to people who either didn't grasp them or dismissed them as impractical. Most of the time, he was met with polite nods or skepticism. But when he spoke to Ada about his plans for the Analytical Engine, she didn't just listen—she built on his ideas, pushing them further than even he had considered.

Their friendship began when Ada was still a teenager, and it grew as she deepened her understanding of mathematics and engineering. Babbage had already introduced her to the Difference Engine, his first attempt at a mechanical calculator. But while that machine was designed to perform a single function—solving mathematical tables—the Analytical Engine was something entirely new.

It was not just a calculator. It was programmable.

Babbage had conceived of a machine that could follow a series of instructions, allowing it to solve different types of problems instead of just one. It was an astonishing idea, far ahead of its time. In today's terms, he was designing the first concept of a computer, though no one in the 1800s would have called it that.

The more Ada learned about it, the more fascinated she became.

She wasn't just interested in how the machine
worked mechanically—she wanted to know what it
meant. What could be done with a machine that
could follow instructions? Could it go beyond mathematics? Could it be programmed to think in
different ways? These were questions no one else
was asking.

Babbage saw Ada's potential and treated her as a
true intellectual partner. He sent her notes,
diagrams, and equations, encouraging her to analyze
the designs and challenge his ideas. Unlike many of
his peers, who dismissed her because of her gender,
he recognized that her mind worked differently—
and that difference was valuable.

Then came the project that would define their
collaboration.

In 1842, an Italian mathematician named Luigi
Federico Menabrea wrote a paper about the Analytical Engine. The paper was in French, and a group of
scientists, including Babbage, wanted it translated
into English. Ada was asked to do the translation.

She didn't just translate it.

She expanded it.

While working on the paper, she added her own

notes—pages and pages of them, longer than the original article itself. In those notes, she explained the capabilities of the Analytical Engine in a way no one else had done before. She described how it could follow instructions, process different kinds of data, and even create outputs beyond just numbers.

Most importantly, she included what is now considered the world's first computer program—a detailed set of instructions showing how the Analytical Engine could calculate Bernoulli numbers, a complex sequence used in mathematics.

This was groundbreaking.

Babbage had invented the machine, but it was Ada who fully grasped its potential. She was the first person in history to understand that a machine like this could be programmed to do far more than simple arithmetic.

Their collaboration was intense. They exchanged letters, debated ideas, and refined their understanding of what the Analytical Engine could achieve. Ada's mind moved quickly, drawing connections that even Babbage hadn't considered. She proposed that, given the right programming, the machine could process not just numbers but symbols, patterns, and even music.

No one else saw this future.

Babbage admired her brilliance, but not everyone appreciated her work. The Analytical Engine was never built during their lifetimes. Some people dismissed Ada's writings, believing that because she was a woman, she could not have truly understood the complexity of what she was describing. Others simply thought the machine itself was impractical, too expensive, and too complicated to ever be useful.

But Ada never doubted the importance of the work.

Even as the world moved on, even as people questioned whether machines like the Analytical Engine would ever be possible, she knew that her ideas—her notes, her vision of what machines could become—mattered.

And she was right.

More than a century later, as real computers began to emerge, engineers and scientists looked back at her work and realized that she had predicted the future of programming before anyone else. What started as a friendship between a determined mathematician and an impatient inventor had led to something no one in their time could have predicted: the birth of computer science.

4

WRITING THE FIRST COMPUTER PROGRAM

The Analytical Engine was unlike anything the world had ever seen. It wasn't just a machine for solving equations. It was something new, something that didn't fit into any category that existed at the time.

Charles Babbage had spent years designing the Difference Engine, a mechanical calculator meant to produce error-free mathematical tables. That alone was an ambitious project. But as he worked on it, his ideas kept growing. He started thinking beyond a machine that could only do one thing. What if a machine could be built that wasn't just limited to solving specific equations but could be programmed to solve anything?

This question led him to something far more ambitious—the Analytical Engine.

It was an invention completely ahead of its time, a machine that worked not just with numbers but with instructions. It could be told what to do. It could follow steps, just like modern computers.

The machine was designed to have four main parts, each of them similar to what modern computers have today.

The first part was called the **mill**. This was where all the calculations happened. If the Analytical Engine had ever been built, the mill would have contained thousands of tiny gears, turning in precise patterns to process numbers. It was, in a way, the machine's brain.

Then there was the **store**. This part was where numbers and results were kept until they were needed, like a memory bank. Unlike the Difference Engine, which could only work on one calculation at a time, the Analytical Engine could hold onto information and use it later.

Next came the **control unit**, which told the machine what to do and in what order. It didn't just follow a single operation. It could be programmed to carry out different sequences, depending on the instructions it was given.

And finally, there was the **input and output** system. The Analytical Engine was designed to use punched cards to feed in instructions. These were stiff paper cards with holes punched in different places to represent numbers and commands. When the machine read them, it understood what it was supposed to do. Once a calculation was finished, the results would be printed or recorded.

This idea of punched cards wasn't new. They had already been used in mechanical looms to control the weaving of fabric. But no one had ever thought to use them in a machine for solving problems. Babbage had taken an idea from one industry and applied it to an entirely different one, creating something never seen before.

The machine wasn't just about adding and subtracting anymore. It could handle complex calculations, switch between different operations, and store data to use later. If built, it would have been the most advanced piece of technology in the world.

Ada Lovelace understood that right away.

She saw that the Analytical Engine wasn't just a better calculator. It was something far more powerful. If a machine could be programmed to follow instructions, then in theory, it could be programmed to do anything. It wasn't limited to math—it could process patterns, analyze information, and even create.

Ada's notes on the machine explored this idea in depth. She described how numbers could be used to represent not just quantities but also symbols and letters. She even suggested that, given the right programming, the machine could compose music by following rules of harmony and rhythm.

This was more than just an invention. It was the beginning of something new, something that wouldn't be fully realized until the first real computers were built more than a hundred years later.

Babbage's vision was too advanced for his time. The Analytical Engine was never completed. The technology simply wasn't ready, and the funding never lasted long enough to bring his full design to life. But the ideas behind it—programmable machines, stored memory, and step-by-step instructions—would one day shape the world.

Ada's famous notes

Ada Lovelace wasn't just interested in how the Analytical Engine functioned—she wanted to explain it in a way that made its possibilities clear to others. Most people who looked at Babbage's machine saw a complex device for solving difficult mathematical problems. Ada saw something more.

When she was asked to translate a paper about the Analytical Engine written by an Italian mathematician, Luigi Federico Menabrea, she didn't just translate it. She expanded it. Her notes ended up being three times longer than the original paper itself.

She didn't just describe what the Analytical Engine was designed to do. She explained how it could work, why it mattered, and how it could be used for things beyond just calculating numbers. She wrote about the potential of programming, long before the word "programming" even existed.

Her notes broke down the mechanics of the Analytical Engine in a way that others hadn't done before. She explained the role of its different components—the mill, the store, the punched cards—and how they worked together to process information. But what made her work extraordinary was that she went beyond simply describing the machine.

She included a detailed example—a step-by-step method for programming the Analytical Engine to calculate a series of numbers known as Bernoulli numbers. These numbers, used in complex mathematical formulas, weren't easy to compute by hand. Ada worked out the instructions that the machine would need to follow, organizing them in a way that resembled modern programming languages.

This was more than just a theory. It was an actual algorithm. The first ever written for a machine.

Ada was thinking far ahead of her time. She described the way the Analytical Engine could follow instructions and modify them based on input. She understood that machines like this could process information in a way similar to human reasoning.

She even predicted that, one day, a machine could manipulate symbols and patterns—not just numbers. She suggested that with the right programming, the Analytical Engine could compose music, create art, and do things beyond simple calculations.

No one else had considered this before. Even Babbage, brilliant as he was, had been focused on numbers. Ada saw the deeper potential.

Not everyone took her seriously. Many believed that a woman couldn't have understood such complex ideas. Others thought her ideas about programming were unnecessary because the Analytical Engine itself had never been built. But her notes remained, preserved in scientific journals.

The first-ever algorithm for a machine

Lovelace wrote something no one had ever written before: an algorithm, a precise set of instructions that a machine could follow step by step to solve a problem.

This wasn't just a list of numbers or an idea scribbled in the margins of a notebook. It was a fully developed plan, something that could be fed into a machine to make it perform a task on its own. At the time, no one had ever seen anything like it.

The problem she chose to tackle was the calculation of **Bernoulli numbers**—a complex sequence used in advanced mathematics. These numbers were difficult to compute by hand, requiring long and tedious calculations. The Analytical Engine, however, was designed to handle repetitive processes with complete accuracy.

Ada broke the problem down into a sequence of operations that the machine could understand. She carefully mapped out each step, organizing it into a structure that looked strikingly similar to modern computer code.

Each punched card in the Analytical Engine would represent a different instruction: one for inputting numbers, another for performing calculations, another for storing results. Ada understood how these instructions had to be arranged to make the machine process the Bernoulli numbers in the right order.

This was groundbreaking for one simple reason —it proved that machines could be programmed.

Up until that point, machines had only been designed to perform a single function. A mechanical loom wove fabric, a steam engine powered locomotives, and a clock told time. Machines didn't "think" in any way, and they certainly didn't follow complex instructions.

The Analytical Engine was different. And Ada had just shown the world what it could do.

Her work wasn't just about making calculations faster. She saw beyond mathematics, suggesting that a machine like this could process patterns of any kind—numbers, symbols, even music. If the right instructions were given, a machine could analyze information, predict results, and manipulate data in a way that mimicked human reasoning.

It was a bold idea, one that no one else had fully

grasped. Not even Babbage, the machine's inventor, had put it into words the way Ada did.

Her algorithm is now recognized as the first computer program ever written. It was proof that machines could be more than simple tools. They could be guided by logic, controlled by sequences of instructions, and made to solve problems beyond basic arithmetic.

5

A VISION FOR THE FUTURE

Ada Lovelace understood something that no one else did. While others saw machines as tools for solving math problems, she saw something much bigger. She realized that numbers were just one kind of information—and if a machine could process numbers, then, in theory, it could process anything.

This idea was radical. In the 1800s, machines had one job each. A steam engine powered trains. A loom wove fabric. A printing press put words onto paper. If a machine was built to do something, that was all it could do. But the Analytical Engine was different. It wasn't designed for just one function. It could be programmed to follow instructions, changing what it did depending on the task.

That changed everything.

Ada saw that the Analytical Engine wasn't just a calculator. It was a processor of information. And information came in many forms. If numbers could be fed into the machine, then what about symbols? Letters? Sounds? Could a machine like this compose music? Could it analyze patterns and recognize relationships? Could it create?

These were ideas no one had ever voiced before. Not even Charles Babbage, who had invented the machine, had gone this far.

In her famous notes, Ada described how the Analytical Engine could manipulate symbols in a way that went beyond math. She wrote that the machine "might act upon other things besides number" and that its true power lay in the way it could be given different sets of instructions.

She even speculated that, with the right programming, the machine could compose music. Music, after all, followed mathematical patterns. Notes had frequencies, rhythms had sequences, and harmonies followed rules. If a machine could be programmed to recognize those patterns, why couldn't it generate a melody?

This was more than just speculation. She was laying the groundwork for something that wouldn't exist for another hundred years—the idea that machines could do more than just compute.

Today, computers do exactly what Ada described. They don't just solve equations; they create art, write stories, and compose music. They process language, analyze data, and recognize images. Every time a computer plays a song, corrects spelling, or generates a digital painting, it is following the same fundamental ideas that Ada Lovelace first wrote about.

Predicting artificial intelligence

Ada Lovelace didn't just think about machines in a way no one else did—she also questioned what they might one day become. While others saw gears and levers designed to crunch numbers, she wondered if a machine could ever do more than just follow instructions. Could it ever think for itself? Could it make decisions? Could it, in some way, mimic human intelligence?

These were questions no one else in the 1800s was asking. Computers didn't exist yet, and even the idea of programmable machines was considered strange. But Ada's mind worked differently. She looked at Babbage's Analytical Engine and saw its potential, not just for calculations but for something much bigger—the ability to process information in ways that had never been done before.

She wrote about these ideas in her notes, carefully considering what the machine could and could not do. She explained that the Analytical Engine, if built, could follow a set of instructions to manipulate symbols and solve problems beyond just mathematics. It could process patterns, store data, and even be programmed to change its course of action based on input.

But then she made a distinction—one that would later become one of the most important discussions in computer science.

She argued that while machines could follow complex instructions, they could not originate thought on their own. They could process information but not think independently. They could execute commands but not create ideas. She wrote, "The Analytical Engine has no pretensions to originate anything. It can do whatever we know how to order it to perform."

This was a groundbreaking statement.

She was describing the limits of computers before computers even existed. And in doing so, she also introduced an idea that would later shape the study of artificial intelligence—could machines ever go beyond their programming? Could they ever truly think?

Today, this question is at the heart of AI research. Scientists and engineers build machines that learn from data, recognize patterns, and make decisions. Some programs can write stories, generate artwork, and even hold conversations. They follow rules, just as Ada described, but the question remains—do they truly understand, or are they just incredibly advanced pattern-recognition tools?

Ada Lovelace predicted this debate long before computers became a reality. She was the first to think critically about the difference between machines that follow instructions and machines that might one day develop something more—intelligence, creativity, independent thought.

How people didn't believe her ideas at the time

Most people in the 1800s couldn't even grasp the concept of a machine that could be programmed, let alone one that could create. To them, machines were tools, nothing more. A steam engine powered a locomotive, a printing press copied words, and a mechanical loom wove fabric. Every machine had a single purpose, and the idea of a machine that could be reprogrammed to perform multiple tasks was, to most, unnecessary—even ridiculous.

Even Charles Babbage, the man who had designed the Analytical Engine, didn't completely follow where Ada's ideas were leading. He had spent years perfecting his vision of a mechanical calculator, but he hadn't thought about it as anything more than an advanced mathematical tool. Ada, on the other hand, saw it as the beginning of something entirely new.

When she wrote her notes on the Analytical Engine, she didn't just explain how it worked—she explored what it could become. Her notes included the first algorithm ever written for a machine, proving that it could be programmed to follow steps and solve problems. She also predicted that machines like this could one day manipulate symbols, compose music, and analyze information in ways that resembled human thought.

Most people weren't ready for that idea.

Mathematicians and engineers of the time read her work, but they didn't understand its importance. Many saw it as an interesting theoretical exercise, nothing more. Some even dismissed it entirely, believing that Ada had overestimated what the Analytical Engine could do.

Part of the problem was that the Analytical Engine itself was never built. Babbage's design was ahead of its time, and the technology to construct it simply didn't exist yet. Without a working machine to prove Ada's ideas, people had little reason to take them seriously.

And then there was the issue of who Ada was.

She was a woman in a time when women were not expected to contribute to mathematics or science. Many of the scholars who read her work were hesitant to give her credit, believing that such advanced thinking could only come from a man. Some assumed that Babbage must have been the true author of her ideas, despite the fact that Ada's notes went far beyond anything he had written.

Even those who acknowledged her work didn't see the full value of it. They viewed her algorithm as an interesting experiment, but they failed to grasp its significance. The world wasn't ready to think about machines the way Ada had.

For years, her ideas were ignored. The Analytical Engine was forgotten, and Ada's work faded into history.

But time had a way of proving her right.

A century later, when computers were finally being developed, scientists rediscovered Ada's notes. They realized that she had described the fundamental principles of programming long before anyone else. She had seen the future of computing before computers even existed.

6

THE CHALLENGES ADA FACED

In the 1800s, women weren't encouraged to study science or mathematics. In fact, many people believed that women's brains weren't suited for complex thinking. Schools didn't teach advanced subjects to girls, and universities didn't admit them. Women were expected to focus on running households, raising children, and entertaining guests.

Ada was different.

Her mother had made sure she had the best tutors and the strongest education possible, but even with that, she was still an outsider in the world of mathematics. The people working in science and engineering—people like Charles Babbage and Augustus De Morgan—were all men. They debated theories, exchanged letters, and worked together on projects, but women were almost never part of the conversation.

Ada had to push her way in.

She had to prove, again and again, that she wasn't just a student of mathematics—she was a thinker, a contributor, someone who could come up with new ideas and challenge the ones that already existed. She had to show that she wasn't just learning for the sake of learning but that she had something valuable to add.

And she did.

When she wrote her famous notes on the Analytical Engine, she wasn't just explaining Babbage's work—she was expanding on it, seeing possibilities that even he hadn't considered. But even after all her effort, many of the scholars reading her work didn't take it seriously.

Some dismissed her ideas outright. They thought she was exaggerating what the Analytical Engine could do. Others assumed that Babbage must have been the true mind behind her notes, even though she had written them herself.

Ada never stopped pushing forward, but the obstacles were constant. Even the most brilliant ideas could be ignored when they came from a woman. She was respected in certain circles, but she was never fully accepted in the way her male counterparts were.

That didn't stop her from shaping the future.

Health struggles

Ada Lovelace had a mind that never stopped working, but her body did not always keep up. From a young age, she struggled with health problems that affected her ability to study, write, and even move.

When she was just a child, she became seriously ill with measles. It was not the kind of mild case that some children recovered from quickly. This illness left her weak and bedridden for months. For a time, she was even paralyzed, unable to walk. It was a terrifying experience. She had always been curious about the world, always moving, always thinking. Being stuck in bed, unable to explore or study the way she wanted, was frustrating.

But Ada's mind did not rest.

Even when she was too weak to sit up for long, she found ways to keep learning. Her mother, who had always been strict about Ada's education, continued to make sure she studied, even when she was sick. Tutors visited her bedside, bringing books and lessons.

She could not run or play the way other children did, but she could read. She could think. She could fill her mind with knowledge, even when her body was too weak to do much else.

Over time, she regained her strength, but she was never entirely free from illness. Throughout her life, she had periods of severe pain, weakness, and exhaustion. Some days, she could work for hours, completely focused on her studies and ideas. Other days, she could do almost nothing.

This unpredictability made her work even more challenging. She had to take advantage of the times when she felt well, pushing herself to write, study, and correspond with the greatest minds of her time. She knew her moments of energy were precious, and she used them to their fullest.

But pushing herself had its costs.

She often worked late into the night, writing out long, detailed mathematical notes, even when she was in pain. She refused to slow down, even when her body told her to. Her letters to Charles Babbage were filled with enthusiasm, curiosity, and deep thought, but there were also hints of frustration. She wanted to do more. She wanted to build on her ideas, develop new theories, and contribute even more to the world of mathematics.

Her health, however, had other plans.

As she grew older, her illnesses became worse. The pain she had dealt with in childhood returned with more intensity. By her mid-thirties, she was in constant discomfort. Even though medicine at the time was limited, doctors tried different treatments, including bloodletting and opium-based medications. The treatments often made her feel worse rather than better.

Despite everything, she kept working as much as she could. She never let illness take away her passion for learning, even when it took away her strength.

Her final years were some of her most difficult. The pain was relentless, and there were fewer and fewer days when she felt strong enough to focus on her studies. But even then, her mind remained sharp. She still thought about numbers, still dreamed of what machines could become, still believed in the future of computing long before anyone else did.

Her health struggles shaped the way she worked, but they never stopped her. Even when her body failed her, her ideas remained powerful—strong enough to change the world, long after she was gone.

Why her work wasn't recognized in her lifetime

Ada Lovelace saw the future, but the world wasn't ready to see it with her.

She had written the first algorithm, the first detailed set of instructions that could be fed into a machine to perform a task on its own. She had explained how the Analytical Engine could do more than just crunch numbers—it could follow commands, store data, and even process patterns in ways that hinted at modern computing. She had predicted that machines could be used for music, language, and ideas, not just math.

But hardly anyone paid attention.

There were many reasons for this, but one of the biggest was that the Analytical Engine itself was never built. Charles Babbage had designed it, refined it, and fought to get the funding to construct it, but the technology of the time wasn't advanced enough to make it a reality. The machine was enormous—if it had been completed, it would have filled an entire room, with thousands of delicate gears and levers working together in perfect sequence.

Building it required money, precision, and a level of engineering skill that simply didn't exist yet. The British government had funded Babbage's earlier work on the Difference Engine, but they lost patience with him when he abandoned it for the even more ambitious Analytical Engine. No machine meant no proof that Ada's ideas could work. And without proof, people dismissed them.

Another reason Ada's work went unrecognized was that most people simply couldn't understand it. Her notes were not just about how the Analytical Engine functioned but about its potential—about what machines could become. This was a time when even basic mechanical inventions were seen as groundbreaking. Steam power had revolutionized transportation, but the idea of a programmable machine? That was too far ahead of its time.

Many of the scientists and mathematicians who read Ada's notes appreciated the technical explanations, but they ignored her theories about computers being able to process more than just numbers. They thought she was overreaching, making claims that weren't grounded in reality. To them, machines were tools, nothing more.

Then there was the fact that Ada was a woman.

In the 1800s, women weren't expected to

contribute to science, math, or engineering. Even the most intelligent and well-educated women were often dismissed when they tried to enter these fields. Men controlled the universities, the scientific journals, and the academic societies. Women were rarely seen as equals in intellectual circles.

Ada had access to education because of her wealth and status, but even that didn't grant her the same respect as her male counterparts. Some believed that Charles Babbage had written most of her notes, despite the fact that she had expanded on his ideas in ways he never had. Others ignored her work entirely, assuming that, because it came from a woman, it couldn't be significant.

Her contributions remained buried in scientific journals, unnoticed and unappreciated.

She had spent her life developing ideas that would one day change the world, but during her lifetime, few people recognized what she had accomplished. There were no awards, no celebrations, no major acknowledgments of what she had done. When she died at just 36 years old, her work seemed to fade with her.

7

THE LEGACY OF ADA LOVELACE

A da Lovelace didn't live to see computers become a reality, but the ideas she wrote about in the 1800s helped shape the technology we rely on today. She had looked at a mechanical machine made of gears and levers and saw something more—a machine that could be programmed to follow instructions, store information, and process symbols.

It took more than a hundred years for the world to catch up to her thinking.

In the 1930s and 1940s, engineers and mathematicians started developing the first electronic computers. These machines weren't made of brass and steel like Babbage's designs, but they followed the same basic principles. They used instructions to process information. They could solve different types of problems instead of just one.

The people building these early computers needed a way to tell them what to do. They needed a system of commands—a way to program the machines to follow a set of steps, just as Ada had described in her notes on the Analytical Engine.

Her ideas were suddenly relevant again.

One of the first people to recognize the importance of her work was Alan Turing, a British mathematician and computer scientist. He is best known for breaking the German Enigma code during World War II, but he also played a huge role in developing the concept of modern computers.

Turing believed that machines could be programmed to do more than just calculate numbers. He argued that computers could process language, logic, and even artificial intelligence—ideas that sounded incredibly similar to what Ada had written a century earlier.

In fact, Turing directly referenced her work when discussing how computers could be designed to follow instructions. He built on her theories, proving that machines could execute a series of commands automatically, just as she had predicted.

As computer programming developed, Ada's

ideas became even more influential. In the 1970s, a new programming language was created, designed for reliability and efficiency. It was named **Ada** in her honor. This language was used in everything from military systems to air traffic control, proving just how far-reaching her influence had become.

Why she is now called the first computer programmer

Ada Lovelace lived in a time before computers existed. There were no screens, no keyboards, and no digital code. And yet, she is remembered today as the world's first computer programmer.

That title comes from something she wrote—a set of detailed instructions for a machine that was never even built. It wasn't just any set of instructions, though. It was the first algorithm designed for a machine to follow, step by step, in order to complete a task.

That's what programming is.

A computer doesn't think for itself. It follows commands. It processes information in a specific way, based on the instructions it has been given. Every program, from the ones that power video games to the ones that control satellites, is built on carefully written steps that tell a machine what to do.

Ada was the first person to write those kinds of instructions.

Her program was designed for the Analytical Engine, Charles Babbage's machine. While Babbage had created the concept of a mechanical computer, he had only thought of it as a tool for solving mathematical problems. Ada took it a step further. She described how it could be programmed to follow a sequence of operations. She wrote out an example, showing how it could be used to calculate Bernoulli numbers—a complicated sequence in mathematics.

This was different from simply using a machine to add and subtract. She had created a process, an organized system of commands that could be fed into the machine to make it work. She had written what we now call an algorithm.

At the time, no one realized how important this was. Most people dismissed her work because they didn't understand what she was trying to do. The Analytical Engine itself was never completed, so her program was never tested. Her ideas were written down, printed in a journal, and then mostly forgotten.

More than a hundred years later, when real

computers were being invented, scientists and engineers looked back at Ada's notes. They realized that she had been describing the core concepts of computer programming long before anyone else had. She had understood that machines could be programmed with instructions to complete tasks automatically.

That is why she is now called the first computer programmer. She didn't just write about a machine —she wrote the first program for one. She saw something no one else did, and her work helped shape the future of technology.

Ada Lovelace Day

Ada Lovelace's ideas were ahead of her time, but today, she is celebrated around the world. Every year, people honor her achievements on **Ada Lovelace Day**, a day dedicated to recognizing the contributions of women in science, technology, engineering, and mathematics—fields often called **STEM**.

This wasn't always the case. For many years after her death, Ada's work was largely forgotten. Her notes sat in scientific journals, unread and unappreciated. The world moved forward without realizing that she had already described the basic ideas of computer programming long before computers existed.

Then, more than a century later, her work was rediscovered.

As computers became a reality in the 20th century, engineers and scientists looked back at her writings and recognized their importance. She had written about algorithms before programming languages existed. She had predicted a future where machines could process more than just numbers. The ideas she had written down in the 1800s had finally caught up with the modern world.

This realization sparked a movement to celebrate Ada's contributions and highlight the importance of women in STEM. In 2009, Ada Lovelace Day was established as a way to encourage girls and women to pursue careers in science, technology, engineering, and mathematics.

Across the world, schools, universities, and companies host events to honor her legacy. Scientists give talks, students learn about her work, and organizations highlight the achievements of women in STEM fields. It's a day to recognize both how far the world has come and how much work still needs to be done.

Even today, women in STEM face challenges. For a long time, science and technology were seen as fields meant for men. Women who wanted to become engineers, programmers, or mathematicians were often discouraged or not taken seriously—just as Ada had been.

Ada Lovelace Day is a reminder that brilliant minds belong in every field, no matter their gender. It encourages young girls to explore science and math, to ask big questions, and to see that they, too, can shape the future.

8

FUN FACTS AND ACTIVITIES

One of the most unusual facts about Ada's life is that she was the daughter of the famous poet Lord Byron. While Ada became known for her work in mathematics, her father was one of the most well-known poets of the Romantic era. He was dramatic, adventurous, and often reckless. His poetry was filled with passion and wild emotions—nothing like the world of numbers and logic that Ada would come to love.

Despite this connection, Ada never really knew her father. He left England shortly after she was born, and she never saw him again. Her mother, Lady Byron, did everything she could to keep Ada from following in his footsteps, filling her education with strict lessons in math and science instead of poetry.

But Ada wasn't only interested in numbers—she also had a creative side. She once developed a fascination with **flight** and spent time studying the way birds moved. She even wrote a book called "**Flyology**," where she explored the mechanics of flying and how machines might be built to mimic bird wings. She sketched out ideas for flying machines long before airplanes were invented.

She was also known for her **bold personality**. Unlike many women of her time, Ada spoke her mind and wasn't afraid to challenge people's ideas. When she worked with Charles Babbage, she didn't just accept what he said—she questioned his designs, offered her own insights, and expanded on his work. Even though she admired him, she was never just his student; she was a true collaborator.

Another little-known part of Ada's life was her **interest in gambling**. She became fascinated with the mathematical patterns behind betting and spent time trying to develop a system that could predict the outcomes of horse races. She believed that numbers could be used to find patterns that others couldn't see. Unfortunately, her efforts didn't lead to success, and she ended up losing money instead of winning it.

Her confidence and ambition sometimes surprised people, especially because she was working in a world dominated by men. Many of her teachers, including the famous mathematician Augustus De Morgan, were amazed by her abilities. He even compared her mind to some of the greatest mathematicians in history, though he also expressed doubt about whether a woman should be studying such advanced topics.

Ada's legacy continues today in ways she never could have predicted. The **U.S. Department of Defense** created a computer programming language in the 1970s and named it "**Ada**" in her honor. It is still used in critical systems like air traffic control, military technology, and medical devices.

Her final request before she died was unusual— she asked to be buried next to the father she never knew, Lord Byron. Despite her mother's efforts to distance her from him, Ada seemed to feel a connection to the man whose words had captured the world's attention, just as her own ideas would one day shape the future.

Simple coding activity for kids to try

Activity: Programming a Robot Friend
What You'll Need:

- A friend, parent, or sibling to act as the "robot"
- A small object (like a toy or a cup)
- Paper and a pencil to write your code

How It Works:

Your job is to write a set of instructions—just like a computer program—that will tell your "robot" how to pick up the object and move it to a new place. But there's a catch: the robot will only do exactly what the instructions say. If your instructions aren't clear, the robot might do something unexpected!

Step 1: Writing Your Code

Think about every tiny step that a person needs to take in order to pick up an object and move it. You can't just say, "Pick up the cup," because a real computer wouldn't know how. You have to break it down into smaller commands.

Here's an example:

1. Move forward 2 steps.

2. Stop.

3. Reach out right hand.

4. Open fingers.

5. Lower hand until fingers touch object.

6. Close fingers around object.

7. Lift hand up.

8. Turn left.

9. Walk forward 3 steps.

10. Stop.

11. Open fingers to drop the object.

Step 2: Running the Program

Give your written instructions to your "robot" and let them follow each step exactly as written. If they run into a problem—like their hand missing the object—it means the code needs to be fixed!

Step 3: Debugging

In programming, fixing mistakes is called **debugging.** If your robot didn't pick up the object correctly, go back and look at the steps. Maybe you forgot to tell them to bend their fingers all the way or to lift their hand before turning. Adjust the instructions and try again.

Step 4: Experimenting

Once you've successfully moved the object, try making the code more efficient. Can you do it in fewer steps? What happens if you change the order of the commands? Could you make a loop where the robot repeats a motion without having to write it out every time?

How to celebrate Ada Lovelace's contributions today

One way to celebrate Ada Lovelace is by **participating in Ada Lovelace Day**, which happens every October. This day is dedicated to recognizing the achievements of women in STEM (science, technology, engineering, and mathematics). Schools, universities, and organizations hold events where people can learn about women in these fields, explore careers in science and technology, and even try coding activities.

Another way to celebrate her legacy is by **learning to code.** Ada was the first person to write a computer program, even before computers existed. Her work showed that machines could follow instructions to solve problems, just like modern computers do today. Trying a simple coding project —like programming a robot friend, writing a basic computer script, or using coding apps like Scratch— can be a fun way to follow in her footsteps.

Reading about **women in science and technology** is also a great way to recognize Ada's impact. She paved the way for future generations of female scientists, engineers, and programmers. Today, women work in every area of STEM, designing space missions, developing new medicines, and creating artificial intelligence. Learning about their stories and contributions helps continue the work Ada started.

Encouraging more girls to explore STEM is another way to honor her. In Ada's time, women weren't expected to study science or math, and even today, fewer girls pursue careers in technology. Supporting science clubs, coding workshops, or mentorship programs for young girls can help change that. Ada showed that great ideas come from anywhere, and every person, no matter their gender, should have the opportunity to learn and create.

Another way to celebrate is by **visiting museums or exhibits about Ada and early computing.** Some science museums have displays about the history of computers, including replicas of Babbage's Analytical Engine and information about Ada's contributions. Seeing how far technology has come since her time makes her work even more impressive.

Even something as simple as **talking about Ada**

Lovelace's story can help keep her legacy alive. She didn't get the recognition she deserved during her lifetime, but today, people know her as the first computer programmer. Sharing her story helps others learn about how she helped shape the world of modern computing.

CONCLUSION: THE POWER OF IMAGINATION AND CURIOSITY

Math, science, and coding aren't just subjects in school—they're the building blocks of how the world works. They shape everything from video games and space travel to medicine and artificial intelligence. Ada Lovelace understood this long before anyone else, and today, encouraging kids to explore these fields means opening doors to endless possibilities.

One of the best ways to make math, science, and coding exciting is to show how they connect to everyday life. Math isn't just about numbers on a page—it's in the way buildings stand tall, how music is composed, and even in the patterns of nature. Science explains how the universe works, from the way plants grow to the way rockets launch into space. Coding powers apps, websites, and even the animations in movies.

Curiosity is the key. Kids naturally ask big questions—why is the sky blue? How do airplanes stay in the air? What makes a computer program work? Encouraging those questions, instead of just giving simple answers, helps build a mindset of discovery. Exploring math and science doesn't mean just memorizing facts; it means experimenting, testing ideas, and thinking critically.

Hands-on activities make learning even more exciting. Science experiments, math puzzles, and coding challenges turn abstract ideas into real experiences. Building a simple bridge out of toothpicks and testing its strength teaches engineering. Creating a code that makes a character move on a screen shows how programming turns ideas into action.

There are many tools available to help kids explore coding. Websites like **Scratch**, **Tynker**, and **Code.org** allow kids to create their own interactive stories, games, and animations. Even younger children can start learning basic coding logic through block-based programming, where they drag and connect instructions instead of writing complicated code.

Math can be fun beyond the classroom, too. Board games, card games, and even video games often use logic, strategy, and numbers. Puzzles like Sudoku or logic riddles challenge the brain in a way that makes problem-solving exciting. When kids see math as something that helps them win a game or solve a mystery, they start to view it differently.

Encouraging kids to explore science can be as simple as looking at the stars or growing a plant. Learning about famous scientists like Marie Curie, Nikola Tesla, or Ada Lovelace shows how curiosity leads to discoveries. Science museums, space documentaries, and interactive apps help bring complex topics to life.

Parents, teachers, and mentors play a big role in encouraging kids to explore STEM. Sometimes, all it takes is telling a child, "You'd be great at this" or "That's a smart way to think about it." Ada Lovelace was encouraged to study math even when most people believed women didn't belong in the field. That encouragement made a difference, just like it can for kids today.

Every invention, every new discovery, and every piece of technology started with a question. Encouraging kids to explore math, science, and coding isn't just about preparing them for the future—it's about showing them that they have the power to shape it.

The importance of creativity in technology

Technology and creativity might seem like opposites, but they go hand in hand. Every great invention, every new piece of software, every advancement in science and engineering starts with an idea—an idea that takes creativity to develop.

Ada Lovelace understood this better than most. She wasn't just skilled in math and logic; she had a unique way of thinking that blended numbers with imagination. When she studied Charles Babbage's Analytical Engine, she didn't just see a machine that could calculate numbers—she saw something that could process patterns, create, and even compose music. That leap of thought required more than just math skills. It required creativity.

Technology is built on problem-solving, and solving problems often means thinking in new ways. Programmers don't just write code—they design systems that help people communicate, play, learn, and explore. Engineers don't just build—they create things that didn't exist before. Scientists don't just follow formulas—they ask big questions and figure out new ways to answer them.

Every app, every video game, every website is a combination of logic and creativity. A game developer needs to know how to code, but they also need to design exciting levels, characters, and challenges. A robotics engineer needs to understand circuits and mechanics, but they also have to think creatively about how their robot will function in the real world.

Music, art, and storytelling all connect to technology, too. Special effects in movies, digital paintings, and animation all rely on computer programs. Even music can be created using algorithms, following patterns of rhythm and harmony just like Ada Lovelace predicted.

Thinking creatively helps people come up with better solutions. If someone is coding an app to help people learn a new language, they need to think about more than just how the code works. They have to ask: What will make this fun? What will make it easy to use? How can it be different from what already exists?

Technology moves forward when people combine knowledge with creativity. Some of the biggest inventions in history happened because someone was willing to think differently. Ada Lovelace's creativity helped shape the future of computers. Today, every new idea in technology—from artificial intelligence to space exploration—comes from people who see the world in a new way.

Creativity isn't just for artists or musicians. It's for inventors, scientists, and programmers, too. The best technology doesn't just work—it inspires, challenges, and opens doors to things no one thought possible before.

Final thoughts

Ada Lovelace's story is filled with determination, curiosity, and ideas that were far ahead of her time. She wasn't just someone who studied numbers—she was a person who saw possibilities where no one else did. She looked at a mechanical machine made of gears and levers and realized it could be programmed like a modern computer. She understood that numbers weren't just for solving math problems but could represent music, language, and patterns. Her way of thinking shaped the future, even though she never got to see the impact of her work.

She lived in a world where women weren't

expected to be scientists or mathematicians, yet she refused to let that stop her. She studied with the best teachers, worked alongside brilliant minds, and developed ideas that would later influence the entire field of computing. She wrote the first algorithm ever designed for a machine. Today, we would call it a computer program, but at the time, there wasn't even a word for what she had done.

Her work was ignored for a long time. Most people didn't understand what she had discovered, and because the Analytical Engine was never built, they thought her ideas weren't useful. But ideas don't disappear. Over a century later, scientists and engineers realized that the notes Ada had written described the foundations of computer programming. She had predicted a future that wouldn't exist until long after she was gone.

Her legacy continues today. Every time a programmer writes code, every time a computer follows a set of instructions, every time technology is used to create something new, it connects back to the ideas Ada Lovelace first explored. The programming language **Ada** was named in her honor, and Ada Lovelace Day is celebrated every year to recognize women in science and technology.

She proved that creativity and logic aren't opposites—they work together to build the future. She showed that science and math aren't just about solving problems, but about thinking in new ways. Her story reminds us that great discoveries start with a question, a different way of looking at the world, and the courage to believe in ideas that others can't yet see.

Made in the USA
Monee, IL
27 March 2025

14733183R00056